Table of Contents

- Chapter 1: Introduction to Edge AI 3
  - What is Edge AI? 3
  - Importance of Real-Time Processing 4
  - Applications of Edge AI 5
- Chapter 2: Edge AI for Autonomous Drones 7
  - Advantages of Edge AI in Autonomous Drones 7
  - Challenges and Solutions 9
  - Case Studies 11
- Chapter 3: Edge AI for Industrial Robots 12
  - Enhancing Efficiency with Edge AI 12
  - Implementing Edge AI in Manufacturing 14
  - Future Trends 15
- Chapter 4: Edge AI for Smart Home Devices 17
  - Smart Home Automation with Edge AI 17
  - Security and Privacy Concerns 18
  - Consumer Adoption 20
- Chapter 5: Edge AI for Wearables 21
  - Monitoring Health and Fitness 21
  - Personalized User Experience 22
  - Integration with IoT Ecosystem 24
- Chapter 6: Edge AI for Healthcare Monitoring Devices 26
  - Remote Patient Monitoring 26
  - Predictive Analytics for Healthcare 27
  - Regulatory Considerations 29
- Chapter 7: Edge AI for Agricultural Drones 30
  - Precision Farming with Edge AI 31
  - Crop Monitoring and Analysis 32
  - Environmental Impact 34
- Chapter 8: Edge AI for Retail Analytics 35

    Improving Customer Experience 35

    Inventory Management 37

    Personalized Marketing Strategies 38

Chapter 9: Edge AI for Predictive Maintenance in Manufacturing 40

    Preventing Downtime with Edge AI 40

    Predictive Maintenance Algorithms 42

    Cost Savings and Efficiency 43

Chapter 10: Edge AI for Traffic Management Systems 45

    Smart Cities and Edge AI 45

    Traffic Flow Optimization 46

    Real-Time Decision Making 48

Chapter 11: Edge AI for Cybersecurity on IoT Devices 49

    Securing IoT Networks with Edge AI 49

    Threat Detection and Prevention 51

    Compliance and Best Practices 52

Chapter 12: Conclusion and Future Outlook 54

    Key Takeaways 54

    Emerging Trends in Edge AI 56

    Recommendations for Professionals in the Field 57

Chapter 1: Introduction to Edge AI

What is Edge AI?

Edge AI, short for Edge Artificial Intelligence, refers to the practice of running AI algorithms locally on devices rather than relying on cloud computing. This approach is crucial for applications that require real-time processing, such as autonomous vehicles, smart cameras, and IoT devices. By processing data at the edge, near the source of the data, Edge AI reduces latency and bandwidth usage, making it ideal for scenarios where immediate decision-making is critical.

One of the key applications of Edge AI is in autonomous drones. These drones need to process vast amounts of data in real-time to navigate safely and make split-second decisions. By running AI algorithms locally on the drone itself, Edge AI enables autonomous drones to react quickly to changing environments and obstacles, without relying on a constant connection to the cloud.

Industrial robots are another area where Edge AI is revolutionizing the way machines interact with their environment. By embedding AI algorithms directly into the robot's hardware, manufacturers can improve the robot's decision-making capabilities, leading to more efficient and reliable operations on the factory floor. Edge AI enables industrial robots to adapt and learn from their surroundings, increasing productivity and reducing downtime.

Smart home devices, such as thermostats, security cameras, and voice assistants, also benefit from Edge AI. By processing data locally on the device, these smart home devices can respond quickly to user commands and changes in the environment, without needing to send data back and forth to the cloud. This not only improves the user experience but also enhances the privacy and security of personal data.

Overall, Edge AI has a wide range of applications across various industries, from healthcare monitoring devices to agricultural drones, retail analytics to traffic management systems, and cybersecurity on IoT devices. By bringing AI capabilities to the edge, professionals can leverage real-time processing to make faster, more accurate decisions, leading to improved efficiency, safety, and performance in their respective fields.

Importance of Real-Time Processing

Real-time processing is a critical component of edge AI, particularly for applications that require immediate decision-making. In industries such as autonomous vehicles, smart cameras, and IoT devices, real-time processing is essential for ensuring efficient and timely operations. By running AI algorithms locally on devices rather than relying on cloud computing, edge AI reduces latency and bandwidth usage, making it ideal for scenarios where quick responses are vital.

One of the key benefits of real-time processing in edge AI is its impact on autonomous vehicles. By enabling vehicles to make split-second decisions based on real-time data, edge AI can significantly improve safety and efficiency on the road. From detecting obstacles to predicting traffic patterns, real-time processing plays a crucial role in ensuring the smooth operation of autonomous vehicles.

In the realm of industrial robots, real-time processing is equally important for optimizing performance and productivity. By processing data locally on the robot itself, edge AI can enable robots to react quickly to changes in their environment, leading to more precise and efficient operations. This real-time processing capability is essential for industries that rely on robotic automation for manufacturing and production processes.

For smart home devices, real-time processing powered by edge AI can enhance the overall user experience by enabling devices to respond instantly to user commands. From adjusting lighting and temperature settings to controlling security systems, real-time processing ensures that smart home devices can react in real-time to changes in their surroundings. This capability not only improves convenience for users but also enhances the efficiency and effectiveness of smart home ecosystems.

In conclusion, real-time processing is a crucial aspect of edge AI that is essential for a wide range of applications across various industries. From autonomous vehicles to industrial robots, smart home devices to healthcare monitoring devices, real-time processing powered by edge AI enables devices to make instant decisions based on real-time data. By reducing latency and bandwidth usage, edge AI enhances the efficiency, safety, and overall performance of devices, making it a valuable technology for professionals in the field.

Applications of Edge AI

In the fast-paced world of technology, applications of Edge AI are becoming increasingly prevalent and essential for various industries. Edge AI involves running AI algorithms locally on devices rather than relying on cloud computing, which is particularly crucial for applications requiring real-time processing. Industries such as autonomous vehicles, smart cameras, and IoT devices benefit greatly from Edge AI as it reduces latency and bandwidth usage, making it suitable for scenarios where immediate decision-making is critical.

One particular application of Edge AI that is gaining traction is in the field of autonomous drones. These drones rely on real-time processing to navigate and make decisions autonomously, making Edge AI a perfect fit for this technology. Edge AI enables drones to react quickly to changing environments and obstacles, ensuring safe and efficient operation.

Industrial robots are another area where Edge AI is making a significant impact. By running AI algorithms locally on the robots themselves, manufacturers can improve efficiency and productivity on the factory floor. Edge AI allows industrial robots to make decisions autonomously, reducing the need for constant human intervention and streamlining processes.

Smart home devices are also benefiting from Edge AI, as they require real-time processing for functions such as voice recognition and security monitoring. By incorporating Edge AI into these devices, manufacturers can provide users with a seamless and responsive experience, enhancing the overall functionality and convenience of smart homes.

In the healthcare industry, Edge AI is revolutionizing monitoring devices by enabling real-time processing of vital signs and health data. Wearable devices equipped with Edge AI can provide immediate feedback and alerts to users and healthcare professionals, allowing for early detection of health issues and improved patient outcomes. Edge AI is transforming the way healthcare is delivered, making monitoring devices more effective and efficient.

Overall, the applications of Edge AI are vast and diverse, spanning industries such as agriculture, retail, manufacturing, and cybersecurity. With its ability to provide real-time processing and reduce latency, Edge AI is becoming a critical component in the development of advanced technologies and solutions for professionals across various niches.

Chapter 2: Edge AI for Autonomous Drones

Advantages of Edge AI in Autonomous Drones

Autonomous drones have become increasingly popular in various industries, from agriculture to security to delivery services. These drones are equipped with advanced technologies that allow them to operate independently without human intervention. One of the key technologies that enable autonomous drones to function effectively is Edge AI. By running AI algorithms locally on the drones themselves, rather than relying on cloud computing, Edge AI offers several advantages that are crucial for the success of autonomous drone operations.

One of the main advantages of Edge AI in autonomous drones is reduced latency. In situations where immediate decision-making is critical, such as in emergency response or surveillance operations, minimizing the delay in processing data is essential. By processing data locally on the drone, Edge AI significantly reduces latency, ensuring that the drone can respond quickly to changing conditions in real-time.

Another key benefit of Edge AI in autonomous drones is decreased bandwidth usage. Sending large amounts of data to the cloud for processing can be costly and inefficient, especially in remote or inaccessible areas where connectivity may be limited. Edge AI allows drones to analyze data on board and only transmit the most relevant information, saving bandwidth and ensuring efficient operation even in challenging environments.

Edge AI also enhances the overall security and privacy of autonomous drones. By processing data locally, sensitive information is not transmitted over potentially insecure networks to the cloud. This reduces the risk of data breaches or unauthorized access, protecting both the drone and the data it collects. Additionally, Edge AI enables drones to operate autonomously without relying on external servers, further enhancing their security and reliability.

Furthermore, Edge AI enables autonomous drones to adapt to changing environments and situations more effectively. By running AI algorithms locally, drones can make decisions based on real-time data without the need for constant communication with a central server. This flexibility allows drones to operate in dynamic environments and respond quickly to unexpected events, making them more versatile and efficient in a wide range of applications.

In conclusion, Edge AI plays a crucial role in the success of autonomous drones by reducing latency, decreasing bandwidth usage, enhancing security, and improving adaptability. As the demand for autonomous drones continues to grow across various industries, understanding the advantages of Edge AI in these devices is essential for professionals looking to leverage this technology effectively in their operations. By harnessing the power of Edge AI, autonomous drones can operate more efficiently, securely, and autonomously, paving the way for new and innovative applications in the future.

Challenges and Solutions

One of the biggest challenges in implementing Edge AI is the limited computational power and memory available on edge devices. This can make it difficult to run complex AI algorithms in real-time, especially in applications such as autonomous vehicles or industrial robots where split-second decision-making is crucial. To address this challenge, developers can optimize their algorithms to run efficiently on edge devices by using techniques such as model compression, quantization, and pruning. By reducing the size and complexity of AI models, developers can ensure that they can run smoothly on edge devices without sacrificing performance.

Another challenge in Edge AI is the need to balance accuracy with speed. In applications such as healthcare monitoring devices or agricultural drones, it is important to have high accuracy in AI predictions while also maintaining real-time processing capabilities. To address this challenge, developers can use techniques such as federated learning, which allows AI models to be trained on decentralized data sources without compromising privacy. By training models on edge devices using federated learning, developers can achieve high accuracy while also ensuring fast processing speeds.

Security is also a major concern in Edge AI, especially in applications such as smart home devices or cybersecurity on IoT devices. Edge devices are often vulnerable to attacks due to their limited security features and connectivity to the internet. To address this challenge, developers can implement measures such as encryption, authentication, and secure boot mechanisms to protect data and ensure the integrity of AI algorithms running on edge devices. By prioritizing security in Edge AI applications, developers can build trust with users and ensure the safety of their data.

Interoperability is another challenge in Edge AI, especially in applications such as retail analytics or traffic management systems where multiple devices and systems need to work together seamlessly. To address this challenge, developers can use open standards and protocols to ensure compatibility between different edge devices and platforms. By adopting standardized communication protocols such as MQTT or CoAP, developers can enable seamless data exchange between edge devices and ensure that AI algorithms can work together effectively to achieve common goals.

In conclusion, Edge AI presents unique challenges and opportunities for professionals working in various industries such as autonomous drones, industrial robots, smart home devices, and healthcare monitoring devices. By addressing challenges such as limited computational power, balancing accuracy with speed, ensuring security, and promoting interoperability, developers can unlock the full potential of Edge AI and create innovative solutions that improve real-time processing capabilities in a wide range of applications.

Case Studies

In the subchapter titled "Case Studies" in the book "Edge AI: Real-Time Processing for Professionals," we will explore various real-world examples of how Edge AI is being utilized across different industries. Edge AI involves running AI algorithms locally on devices rather than relying on cloud computing, making it crucial for applications requiring real-time processing. Some of the key niches where Edge AI is making a significant impact include autonomous vehicles, smart cameras, and IoT devices.

One compelling case study is the use of Edge AI for autonomous drones. By processing data locally on the drone itself, it can make split-second decisions without relying on a stable internet connection. This is crucial for applications such as search and rescue missions or aerial surveillance where immediate decision-making is critical.

In the realm of industrial robots, Edge AI is revolutionizing the manufacturing industry. By running AI algorithms on the robot itself, it can adapt to changing conditions in real-time, leading to increased efficiency and productivity. This is particularly important for tasks that require precision and speed, such as assembly line operations.

Smart home devices are another area where Edge AI is making a significant impact. By processing data locally on the device, it can provide personalized and responsive experiences for users. For example, smart thermostats can learn user preferences and adjust the temperature accordingly without relying on cloud computing.

Healthcare monitoring devices are also benefiting from Edge AI technology. By analyzing patient data locally on the device, it can provide real-time insights and alerts for healthcare professionals. This is particularly important for monitoring patients with chronic conditions or those at risk of medical emergencies.

In conclusion, Edge AI is transforming various industries by enabling real-time processing on devices. From autonomous drones to healthcare monitoring devices, the possibilities are endless. By reducing latency and bandwidth usage, Edge AI is making immediate decision-making possible in scenarios where it is critical. As professionals, it is essential to stay updated on the latest advancements in Edge AI to harness its full potential in our respective fields.

Chapter 3: Edge AI for Industrial Robots

Enhancing Efficiency with Edge AI

In the world of artificial intelligence (AI), there is a growing trend towards utilizing edge computing to enhance efficiency and speed. Edge AI involves running AI algorithms locally on devices rather than relying on cloud computing. This is particularly crucial for applications that require real-time processing, such as autonomous vehicles, smart cameras, and IoT devices. By leveraging Edge AI, organizations can reduce latency and bandwidth usage, making it ideal for scenarios where immediate decision-making is critical.

One of the key benefits of Edge AI is its ability to provide real-time processing for autonomous drones. By running AI algorithms locally on the drone itself, organizations can improve the drone's ability to make split-second decisions without relying on a distant cloud server. This can significantly enhance the drone's performance and responsiveness, making it more reliable and efficient in various applications such as surveillance, agriculture, and delivery services.

Industrial robots are another area where Edge AI can greatly enhance efficiency. By processing AI algorithms locally on the robot, organizations can reduce latency and improve the robot's ability to perform complex tasks quickly and accurately. This can lead to increased productivity and cost savings for manufacturing facilities, as well as improved safety and reliability in industrial settings.

Smart home devices are also benefiting from Edge AI technology. By running AI algorithms locally on devices such as smart thermostats, security cameras, and voice assistants, homeowners can enjoy faster response times and improved privacy. Edge AI enables smart home devices to make intelligent decisions without relying on a cloud server, ensuring that personal data stays secure and that devices operate smoothly even in cases of poor internet connectivity.

In conclusion, Edge AI is revolutionizing various industries by enhancing efficiency, reducing latency, and improving decision-making capabilities. From autonomous drones to industrial robots, smart home devices to healthcare monitoring devices, Edge AI is transforming the way organizations leverage AI technology. By embracing Edge AI, professionals can unlock new opportunities for innovation and growth in their respective fields.

Implementing Edge AI in Manufacturing

Implementing Edge AI in manufacturing is a crucial step towards improving efficiency, productivity, and safety in industrial settings. By running AI algorithms locally on devices within the manufacturing environment, companies can reduce latency and make real-time decisions without relying on cloud computing. This is particularly important for applications in manufacturing that require immediate decision-making, such as predictive maintenance, quality control, and process optimization.

One area where Edge AI is making a significant impact in manufacturing is in industrial robots. By equipping robots with AI capabilities at the edge, they can make autonomous decisions and adapt to changing conditions in real-time. This not only improves the efficiency of manufacturing processes but also enhances worker safety by reducing the risk of accidents on the factory floor.

Another key application of Edge AI in manufacturing is in predictive maintenance. By analyzing data from sensors and machinery at the edge, companies can identify potential issues before they cause downtime or costly repairs. This proactive approach to maintenance can save companies time and money by preventing unexpected breakdowns and optimizing equipment performance.

Edge AI is also being used in manufacturing for quality control and defect detection. By deploying AI algorithms on smart cameras and IoT devices at the edge, companies can quickly identify defects in products and ensure that only high-quality items make it to the market. This not only improves product quality but also reduces waste and improves customer satisfaction.

In conclusion, implementing Edge AI in manufacturing is a game-changer for companies looking to improve efficiency, productivity, and safety in their operations. By running AI algorithms locally on devices within the manufacturing environment, companies can make real-time decisions, reduce latency, and optimize processes for better outcomes. Whether it's for predictive maintenance, quality control, industrial robots, or defect detection, Edge AI is revolutionizing the way manufacturing companies operate in today's fast-paced and competitive landscape.

Future Trends

As technology continues to advance, the future of Edge AI is looking brighter than ever. With the ability to run AI algorithms locally on devices rather than relying on cloud computing, Edge AI is becoming increasingly important for applications requiring real-time processing. This is particularly crucial for industries such as autonomous vehicles, smart cameras, and IoT devices, where immediate decision-making is critical. By reducing latency and bandwidth usage, Edge AI is revolutionizing the way these devices operate, making them more efficient and responsive than ever before.

One of the most exciting future trends in Edge AI is its application in autonomous drones. With the ability to process data in real-time, drones can make split-second decisions while in flight, improving their safety and efficiency. Edge AI is also being utilized in industrial robots, allowing them to perform complex tasks with greater precision and speed. This technology is transforming the manufacturing industry, enabling robots to work alongside humans in a more seamless and efficient manner.

In the realm of smart home devices, Edge AI is making homes safer and more convenient. From smart thermostats to security cameras, these devices can now make decisions without needing to connect to the cloud, reducing response times and improving overall performance. Wearables are also benefiting from Edge AI, with devices like fitness trackers and health monitors able to provide real-time insights and alerts to users.

Healthcare monitoring devices are another area where Edge AI is making a significant impact. By processing data locally, these devices can provide more accurate and timely information to healthcare professionals, improving patient outcomes and reducing the burden on the healthcare system. Agricultural drones equipped with Edge AI are revolutionizing the way farmers monitor and manage their crops, leading to increased yields and more sustainable farming practices.

In retail analytics, Edge AI is being used to analyze customer behavior in real-time, allowing retailers to make personalized recommendations and optimize their operations. Predictive maintenance in manufacturing is also benefiting from Edge AI, with machines able to anticipate potential issues before they occur, reducing downtime and maintenance costs. In traffic management systems, Edge AI is helping to improve traffic flow and reduce congestion, while in cybersecurity on IoT devices, it is enhancing security measures and protecting against cyber threats. The future of Edge AI is limitless, with endless possibilities for innovation and growth in a wide range of industries.

Chapter 4: Edge AI for Smart Home Devices

Smart Home Automation with Edge AI

Smart home automation has become increasingly popular in recent years, with more and more homeowners looking to make their living spaces smarter and more efficient. One of the key technologies driving this trend is Edge AI, which involves running AI algorithms locally on devices rather than relying on cloud computing. This is particularly important for applications requiring real-time processing, such as smart home devices, where immediate decision-making is critical.

Edge AI in smart home automation allows for faster response times and reduced latency, as the AI algorithms are processed locally on the devices themselves. This means that smart home devices can make decisions quickly and efficiently without having to rely on a constant internet connection. This is especially beneficial for scenarios where real-time processing is essential, such as home security systems or smart thermostats.

One of the key benefits of using Edge AI in smart home automation is the reduction in bandwidth usage. By processing AI algorithms locally on the devices, less data needs to be sent to the cloud for processing. This not only reduces latency but also helps to lower the overall bandwidth usage, making smart home automation more efficient and cost-effective.

Edge AI can be used in a variety of smart home devices, ranging from smart cameras to smart speakers to smart thermostats. By incorporating Edge AI into these devices, homeowners can enjoy a more seamless and integrated smart home experience. For example, smart cameras can use Edge AI to detect intruders in real-time, while smart thermostats can adjust the temperature based on occupancy patterns detected by Edge AI algorithms.

Overall, Edge AI is revolutionizing the way we think about smart home automation, allowing for faster response times, reduced latency, and more efficient processing of AI algorithms. By incorporating Edge AI into smart home devices, homeowners can enjoy a more connected and intelligent living space that responds to their needs in real-time. With the rise of Edge AI in smart home automation, the possibilities for creating a truly smart and efficient home are endless.

Security and Privacy Concerns

When it comes to implementing Edge AI solutions, one of the primary concerns that professionals need to address is security and privacy. Running AI algorithms locally on devices opens up new vulnerabilities that need to be carefully managed to prevent potential breaches. With Edge AI being utilized in critical applications such as autonomous vehicles, industrial robots, and healthcare monitoring devices, the stakes are high when it comes to protecting sensitive data and ensuring the safety of users.

One of the main security concerns with Edge AI is the risk of unauthorized access to the data being processed on the device. Since the algorithms are running locally, there is a possibility that malicious actors could intercept or manipulate the data, leading to potentially dangerous outcomes. Professionals working with Edge AI need to implement robust encryption methods and access controls to prevent unauthorized access and ensure the integrity of the data being processed.

In addition to security concerns, privacy is also a major issue when it comes to Edge AI. With devices collecting and processing vast amounts of personal data, there is a risk of privacy violations if this data is not properly protected. Professionals need to be aware of the regulations and guidelines surrounding data privacy, such as GDPR, and ensure that they are compliant when deploying Edge AI solutions in sensitive environments.

Furthermore, professionals working with Edge AI need to consider the implications of data sharing and storage. Since Edge AI devices are often connected to the internet or other devices, there is a risk of data leaks if proper security measures are not in place. It is essential for professionals to carefully design their systems to minimize the risk of data breaches and ensure that user data is protected at all times.

Overall, security and privacy concerns are paramount when working with Edge AI solutions. By implementing robust security measures, ensuring compliance with data privacy regulations, and carefully managing data sharing and storage, professionals can minimize the risks associated with running AI algorithms locally on devices. With careful planning and attention to detail, professionals can ensure that their Edge AI solutions are secure, reliable, and privacy-conscious.

Consumer Adoption

Consumer adoption of Edge AI technologies is on the rise, as more and more professionals recognize the benefits of running AI algorithms locally on devices. This approach is particularly crucial for applications requiring real-time processing, such as autonomous vehicles, smart cameras, and IoT devices. By leveraging Edge AI, companies can reduce latency and bandwidth usage, making it ideal for scenarios where immediate decision-making is critical.

One niche where Edge AI is making a significant impact is in autonomous drones. These drones require the ability to make split-second decisions while avoiding obstacles and navigating complex environments. By processing AI algorithms locally on the drone itself, companies can ensure that these decisions are made in real-time, without relying on a connection to the cloud.

Industrial robots are another area where Edge AI is revolutionizing operations. By running AI algorithms directly on the robot, companies can improve efficiency and accuracy in manufacturing processes. This allows for faster decision-making and more precise movements, ultimately leading to increased productivity and cost savings.

Smart home devices are also benefiting from Edge AI technologies. By processing AI algorithms locally on the device, companies can enhance security and privacy, while also improving the device's responsiveness. This is particularly important for devices that rely on real-time data processing, such as smart thermostats or security cameras.

In conclusion, consumer adoption of Edge AI technologies is rapidly increasing across a wide range of industries. From autonomous drones to smart home devices, Edge AI is providing professionals with the tools they need to make real-time decisions and improve operational efficiency. As more companies recognize the benefits of running AI algorithms locally on devices, we can expect to see even greater advancements in Edge AI technologies in the years to come.

Chapter 5: Edge AI for Wearables

Monitoring Health and Fitness

Monitoring health and fitness is a crucial aspect of maintaining a healthy lifestyle, and with the advancements in technology, Edge AI is playing a significant role in revolutionizing how we track and analyze our well-being. By harnessing the power of Edge AI, individuals can now have real-time access to personalized health data without relying on cloud computing, making it ideal for applications requiring immediate decision-making.

One key area where Edge AI is making a significant impact is in the realm of wearable devices. From smartwatches to fitness trackers, these devices leverage Edge AI algorithms to monitor vital signs, track physical activity, and even provide real-time feedback on workouts. This real-time processing capability allows users to stay informed about their health status and make informed decisions on the go.

Healthcare monitoring devices are another sector where Edge AI is transforming the way we monitor and manage our health. With the ability to analyze data locally on the device, healthcare professionals can now access critical information quickly and efficiently, leading to faster diagnosis and treatment. From monitoring chronic conditions to tracking vital signs in real-time, Edge AI is revolutionizing the healthcare industry.

In addition to personal health monitoring, Edge AI is also being utilized in the field of agricultural drones. These drones are equipped with Edge AI algorithms that can analyze crop health, detect pests, and even optimize irrigation practices in real-time. By processing data locally on the drone, farmers can make informed decisions on the spot, leading to increased crop yield and reduced environmental impact.

Overall, the integration of Edge AI in monitoring health and fitness is revolutionizing how we track and analyze our well-being. From wearable devices to healthcare monitoring tools and agricultural drones, Edge AI is enabling real-time processing of data, leading to more efficient decision-making and better outcomes for individuals and industries alike. Whether it's monitoring vital signs or optimizing crop health, Edge AI is paving the way for a healthier and more connected future.

Personalized User Experience

In the realm of Edge AI, providing a personalized user experience is paramount for ensuring the success of applications across various industries. By running AI algorithms locally on devices, Edge AI enables real-time processing that can cater to the specific needs and preferences of individual users. This level of customization is particularly crucial for applications such as autonomous vehicles, smart cameras, and IoT devices, where immediate decision-making is critical. With Edge AI, latency is reduced, and bandwidth usage is optimized, resulting in a seamless and responsive user experience.

Autonomous drones are one of the key areas where personalized user experience is essential. Edge AI allows drones to adapt to changing environments in real-time, ensuring smooth navigation and precise decision-making. By analyzing data locally on the drone itself, personalized features can be implemented to enhance user control and overall performance. This level of customization not only improves the user experience but also increases the efficiency and safety of autonomous drone operations.

Industrial robots also benefit greatly from Edge AI in terms of providing a personalized user experience. By processing data locally on the robot, AI algorithms can adapt to individual tasks and optimize performance based on specific requirements. This level of customization enables industrial robots to work more efficiently and effectively, ultimately leading to increased productivity and cost savings for businesses. With Edge AI, personalized user experiences for industrial robots are not only achievable but also essential for maximizing their potential in various manufacturing environments.

Smart home devices are another area where personalized user experience plays a crucial role. With Edge AI, devices such as smart thermostats, lighting systems, and security cameras can learn user preferences and adapt to individual habits in real-time. This level of personalization not only enhances user convenience and comfort but also improves energy efficiency and overall security in smart homes. By leveraging Edge AI, smart home devices can provide a seamless and tailored user experience that meets the needs and expectations of homeowners.

In conclusion, Edge AI is revolutionizing the way personalized user experiences are delivered across a wide range of industries and applications. By processing data locally on devices, AI algorithms can adapt to individual needs and preferences, resulting in a seamless and responsive user experience. Whether it's autonomous drones, industrial robots, smart home devices, wearables, healthcare monitoring devices, agricultural drones, retail analytics, predictive maintenance in manufacturing, traffic management systems, or cybersecurity on IoT devices,

Edge AI is paving the way for a new era of personalized user experiences that are tailored to meet the demands of modern consumers and businesses alike.

Integration with IoT Ecosystem

Integration with the IoT ecosystem is a crucial aspect of implementing Edge AI solutions. By connecting AI algorithms to IoT devices, businesses can unlock a plethora of opportunities to enhance efficiency, productivity, and overall user experience. This integration allows for real-time processing capabilities, enabling devices to make immediate decisions without relying on cloud computing. This is particularly beneficial for applications requiring quick response times, such as autonomous vehicles, smart cameras, and IoT devices.

Edge AI plays a vital role in various niches within the IoT ecosystem. For example, in the realm of autonomous drones, Edge AI enables these devices to navigate complex environments, avoid obstacles, and make split-second decisions to ensure safe and efficient operation. Similarly, in the industrial robotics sector, Edge AI empowers robots to perform tasks with precision and agility, enhancing productivity in manufacturing and logistics operations.

In the realm of smart home devices, Edge AI can provide personalized experiences for users by analyzing data locally and adjusting settings in real-time. Wearables equipped with Edge AI capabilities can track and analyze health data, providing valuable insights for users and healthcare professionals. In the agriculture industry, Edge AI enables drones to monitor crops, detect pests, and optimize irrigation, leading to increased yields and reduced environmental impact.

Retailers can leverage Edge AI for analytics to gain valuable insights into customer behavior, optimize store layouts, and improve inventory management. In the manufacturing sector, Edge

AI can facilitate predictive maintenance, allowing companies to minimize downtime and reduce maintenance costs. Traffic management systems can benefit from Edge AI by analyzing real-time data to optimize traffic flow, reduce congestion, and enhance safety on the roads.

Overall, integrating Edge AI with the IoT ecosystem opens up a world of possibilities for businesses across various industries. By harnessing the power of real-time processing at the edge, organizations can improve operational efficiency, enhance user experiences, and drive innovation in an increasingly connected world.

Chapter 6: Edge AI for Healthcare Monitoring Devices

Remote Patient Monitoring

Remote Patient Monitoring is a crucial aspect of healthcare that has been revolutionized by the integration of Edge AI technology. By utilizing Edge AI algorithms locally on devices, healthcare professionals are able to monitor patients in real-time without relying on cloud computing. This is particularly important for scenarios where immediate decision-making is critical, such as in emergency situations or for patients with chronic conditions that require constant monitoring.

One of the key benefits of Remote Patient Monitoring with Edge AI is the reduction in latency and bandwidth usage. This means that healthcare professionals can receive data from patients' monitoring devices quickly and efficiently, allowing for timely interventions and adjustments to treatment plans. This real-time processing capability is especially valuable for patients who may require immediate medical attention or for those who need continuous monitoring of vital signs.

In the realm of healthcare monitoring devices, Edge AI has enabled the development of wearable devices that can track a wide range of health metrics in real-time. From monitoring heart rate and blood pressure to detecting irregularities in breathing patterns, these devices provide valuable insights into patients' health status without the need for constant supervision by healthcare professionals. This not only improves the quality of care for patients but also allows for early detection of potential health issues before they escalate.

Furthermore, Remote Patient Monitoring with Edge AI has the potential to transform the way healthcare is delivered to patients in remote or underserved areas. By utilizing Edge AI algorithms on devices such as smartphones or tablets, healthcare providers can remotely monitor patients' health without the need for frequent in-person visits. This not only improves access to healthcare services for patients in remote areas but also reduces the burden on healthcare systems by enabling more efficient allocation of resources.

Overall, the integration of Edge AI technology into Remote Patient Monitoring devices has the potential to revolutionize the way healthcare is delivered and monitored. By providing real-time processing capabilities, reducing latency, and improving access to care for patients in remote areas, Edge AI is poised to significantly impact the healthcare industry and improve patient outcomes.

Predictive Analytics for Healthcare

Predictive analytics has become an essential tool in the healthcare industry, allowing professionals to forecast trends, identify potential risks, and personalize patient care. By harnessing the power of data and artificial intelligence, healthcare providers can make more informed decisions and improve outcomes for their patients. Edge AI plays a crucial role in enabling predictive analytics for healthcare by enabling real-time processing of data on local devices, ensuring that critical information is available instantly when needed.

One area where predictive analytics is making a significant impact is in the monitoring of patients with chronic conditions. By analyzing data from wearable devices and other monitoring tools in real-time, healthcare providers can identify patterns and trends that may indicate an impending health crisis. This early warning system allows for timely intervention and can help prevent serious complications, ultimately improving patient outcomes.

Another application of predictive analytics in healthcare is in the field of personalized medicine. By analyzing a patient's genetic makeup, lifestyle factors, and medical history, healthcare providers can tailor treatment plans to individual patients, maximizing the effectiveness of interventions and reducing the risk of adverse reactions. Edge AI enables this personalized approach by processing data quickly and efficiently, allowing for real-time adjustments to treatment plans as new information becomes available.

In addition to patient care, predictive analytics is also being used to optimize hospital operations and resource allocation. By analyzing data on patient flow, staffing levels, and equipment utilization, healthcare administrators can identify areas for improvement and make data-driven decisions to enhance efficiency and reduce costs. Edge AI enables this real-time analysis, allowing for immediate adjustments to be made to improve overall hospital performance.

Overall, predictive analytics powered by Edge AI has the potential to revolutionize healthcare by enabling more personalized, efficient, and effective care for patients. By harnessing the power of data and artificial intelligence, healthcare providers can anticipate needs, identify risks, and make informed decisions that lead to better outcomes for patients. As technology continues to advance, the possibilities for predictive analytics in healthcare are endless, offering new opportunities to improve the quality of care and ultimately save lives.

Regulatory Considerations

Regulatory considerations play a crucial role in the implementation of Edge AI technologies across various industries. As Edge AI involves processing data locally on devices, it raises important privacy and security concerns that must be addressed to comply with regulations such as GDPR, HIPAA, and CCPA. Companies developing Edge AI solutions must ensure that they are in full compliance with these regulations to protect user data and maintain trust in their products.

In the context of autonomous vehicles, regulatory considerations are paramount for ensuring the safety and reliability of these technologies. Edge AI for autonomous drones must adhere to strict regulations set by aviation authorities to prevent accidents and ensure compliance with airspace regulations. Similarly, Edge AI for industrial robots must meet safety standards to protect workers from potential hazards in manufacturing environments.

Smart home devices powered by Edge AI must comply with data protection regulations to safeguard user privacy. Wearables equipped with Edge AI capabilities must adhere to regulations governing the collection and processing of personal health data to ensure the security and confidentiality of sensitive information. Healthcare monitoring devices leveraging Edge AI must meet stringent regulatory requirements to ensure the accuracy and reliability of medical data.

Agricultural drones utilizing Edge AI technologies must comply with regulations governing the use of drones in agricultural settings, such as restrictions on flight paths and data collection practices. Retail analytics powered by Edge AI must adhere to regulations governing the collection and use of customer data to protect consumer privacy. Predictive maintenance solutions in manufacturing leveraging Edge AI must comply with industry regulations to ensure the safety and efficiency of production processes.

In the realm of traffic management systems, Edge AI technologies must comply with regulations governing the use of traffic data to optimize traffic flow and improve road safety. Cybersecurity measures for IoT devices leveraging Edge AI must meet regulatory requirements to protect against cyber threats and ensure the security of connected devices. By considering regulatory requirements in the development and deployment of Edge AI solutions, professionals can ensure the ethical and compliant use of these technologies across a wide range of industries.

Chapter 7: Edge AI for Agricultural Drones

Precision Farming with Edge AI

Precision farming, also known as precision agriculture, is a farming management concept that utilizes technology to optimize crop yields and reduce waste. With the advancement of Edge AI, precision farming has reached new heights in terms of efficiency and accuracy. Edge AI involves running AI algorithms locally on devices, eliminating the need for cloud computing and reducing latency and bandwidth usage. This is particularly crucial for applications requiring real-time processing, such as autonomous vehicles, smart cameras, and IoT devices.

One of the key applications of Edge AI in precision farming is the use of autonomous drones. These drones are equipped with AI algorithms that can analyze data collected from sensors and cameras in real-time, allowing farmers to monitor crop health, detect diseases, and optimize irrigation and fertilization strategies. By utilizing Edge AI, farmers can make immediate decisions based on accurate and up-to-date information, resulting in higher crop yields and reduced costs.

Another important area where Edge AI is making a significant impact in precision farming is in the realm of agricultural drones. These drones are equipped with AI-powered sensors that can collect data on soil quality, crop health, and environmental conditions. By processing this data locally using Edge AI algorithms, farmers can make informed decisions on planting, harvesting, and pest control, leading to more sustainable and efficient farming practices.

In addition to drones, Edge AI is also being utilized in precision farming for retail analytics. By analyzing data from sensors and cameras in real-time, retailers can optimize inventory management, track customer behavior, and enhance the overall shopping experience. Edge AI enables retailers to make quick and accurate decisions, leading to increased sales and customer satisfaction.

Overall, the integration of Edge AI in precision farming is revolutionizing the way farmers manage their crops and resources. By leveraging real-time processing capabilities, Edge AI enables farmers to make faster and more informed decisions, leading to increased productivity, reduced waste, and improved sustainability. As technology continues to advance, the potential for Edge AI in precision farming is limitless, offering endless possibilities for innovation and growth in the agriculture industry.

Crop Monitoring and Analysis

Crop monitoring and analysis are essential components of precision agriculture, allowing farmers to make data-driven decisions to optimize crop yield and reduce waste. Edge AI plays a crucial role in this process by enabling real-time processing of data collected from sensors and drones in the field. By running AI algorithms locally on devices, farmers can quickly analyze information such as soil moisture levels, crop health, and pest infestations without relying on cloud computing, reducing latency and bandwidth usage.

One application of Edge AI in crop monitoring is autonomous drones equipped with AI algorithms to capture high-resolution images of fields and analyze them on the spot. These drones can identify areas of concern, such as nutrient deficiencies or weed infestations, allowing farmers to take immediate action to address these issues. By leveraging Edge AI for autonomous drones, farmers can improve the efficiency and accuracy of their crop monitoring process, leading to increased yields and reduced costs.

Industrial robots equipped with Edge AI can also play a role in crop monitoring and analysis by automating tasks such as planting, watering, and harvesting. These robots can use AI algorithms to navigate fields, identify crops, and perform targeted actions based on real-time data. By integrating Edge AI into industrial robots, farmers can streamline their operations, increase productivity, and reduce labor costs.

Smart home devices powered by Edge AI can further enhance crop monitoring and analysis by providing farmers with real-time insights and alerts about their crops. For example, smart sensors can collect data on temperature, humidity, and light levels in greenhouses, allowing farmers to adjust environmental conditions to optimize crop growth. By leveraging Edge AI for smart home devices, farmers can improve the precision and efficiency of their crop monitoring efforts, resulting in healthier crops and higher yields.

In conclusion, Edge AI offers a wide range of applications for crop monitoring and analysis, from autonomous drones to industrial robots to smart home devices. By running AI algorithms locally on devices, farmers can make real-time decisions based on data collected from the field, leading to improved crop yield and reduced waste. With the increasing adoption of Edge AI in agriculture, farmers can expect to see significant advancements in precision farming techniques and sustainable practices.

Environmental Impact

The environmental impact of Edge AI technology is a crucial aspect to consider when implementing it in various applications. By running AI algorithms locally on devices, Edge AI reduces the need for constant communication with cloud servers, thus minimizing the energy consumption associated with data transmission. This results in lower carbon emissions and overall energy usage, making Edge AI a more sustainable option for real-time processing needs.

One specific area where the environmental impact of Edge AI is evident is in autonomous vehicles. By enabling vehicles to make split-second decisions locally, Edge AI reduces the reliance on cloud computing and decreases the energy consumption associated with constant data transmission. This not only improves the overall efficiency of autonomous vehicles but also reduces their environmental footprint, making them a more sustainable transportation option for the future.

Similarly, Edge AI plays a significant role in reducing the environmental impact of industrial robots by enabling them to perform complex tasks locally without constant communication with cloud servers. This not only improves the efficiency and speed of industrial processes but also reduces energy consumption and carbon emissions associated with data transmission. As a result, Edge AI technology is becoming increasingly popular in the manufacturing industry for its environmental benefits.

In the realm of smart home devices, Edge AI is revolutionizing the way we interact with our homes while also reducing our environmental impact. By running AI algorithms locally on devices such as smart thermostats and lighting systems, Edge AI enables more efficient energy management and reduces overall energy consumption. This not only saves homeowners money on their utility bills but also benefits the environment by reducing carbon emissions associated with excessive energy usage.

Overall, the adoption of Edge AI technology in various applications is not only beneficial for improving real-time processing capabilities but also for reducing our environmental impact. By enabling devices to make decisions locally and minimizing the need for constant communication with cloud servers, Edge AI is paving the way for a more sustainable future in autonomous vehicles, industrial robots, smart home devices, and other applications. As professionals in the field of Edge AI, it is essential to consider the environmental impact of this technology and strive to implement it in a way that maximizes efficiency while minimizing our carbon footprint.

Chapter 8: Edge AI for Retail Analytics

Improving Customer Experience

In the subchapter titled "Improving Customer Experience" in the book "Edge AI: Real-Time Processing for Professionals," we delve into the ways in which Edge AI can enhance customer satisfaction and overall experience. Edge AI, which involves running AI algorithms locally on devices rather than relying on cloud computing, is particularly crucial for applications requiring real-time processing. This is essential in scenarios such as autonomous vehicles, smart cameras, and IoT devices where immediate decision-making is critical. By leveraging Edge AI, businesses can reduce latency and bandwidth usage, resulting in faster and more efficient customer interactions.

One niche where Edge AI can significantly impact customer experience is in autonomous drones. These drones rely on real-time processing to navigate their surroundings and deliver goods or services. By incorporating Edge AI algorithms directly into the drones, companies can ensure smoother and more accurate deliveries, ultimately improving customer satisfaction. Similarly, in industrial robots, Edge AI can optimize production processes, leading to faster turnaround times and higher-quality products. This, in turn, translates to improved customer experience and increased loyalty.

Another area where Edge AI can revolutionize customer experience is in smart home devices. By embedding AI algorithms directly into these devices, companies can offer personalized and intuitive user experiences. From smart thermostats that adjust to individual preferences to security cameras that detect suspicious activity, Edge AI can enhance the functionality and usability of smart home devices. This level of customization not only delights customers but also fosters brand loyalty and advocacy.

In the healthcare industry, Edge AI plays a crucial role in monitoring devices. By processing data locally on the devices themselves, healthcare providers can deliver real-time insights and alerts to patients, improving their overall experience and well-being. From monitoring vital signs to detecting anomalies, Edge AI can enable proactive and personalized healthcare solutions that prioritize patient comfort and convenience. This, in turn, leads to better health outcomes and increased patient satisfaction.

In conclusion, Edge AI has the power to transform customer experience across various industries, from retail analytics to traffic management systems. By leveraging real-time processing capabilities, businesses can deliver faster, more personalized, and more efficient services to their customers. Whether it's enhancing delivery drones, optimizing industrial processes, or improving smart home devices, Edge AI is revolutionizing the way companies interact with their customers. By prioritizing customer experience and leveraging the capabilities of Edge AI, businesses can stay ahead of the competition and drive growth in the digital age.

Inventory Management

Inventory management is a critical aspect of any business operation, and with the advent of Edge AI technology, it has become even more efficient and effective. Edge AI involves running AI algorithms locally on devices rather than relying on cloud computing, making it particularly suitable for applications requiring real-time processing. This is crucial for industries such as autonomous vehicles, smart cameras, and IoT devices, where immediate decision-making is essential.

One area where Edge AI has shown significant improvements in inventory management is in the realm of autonomous drones. These drones can use Edge AI algorithms to monitor and track inventory levels in warehouses in real time, allowing for quicker and more accurate inventory management. This not only reduces the risk of stockouts or overstocking but also improves overall operational efficiency.

Similarly, Edge AI has also revolutionized inventory management in industrial robots. These robots can now use AI algorithms to optimize their movements and tasks based on real-time data, leading to more efficient production processes and reduced downtime. This has a direct impact on inventory management, as it ensures that materials are used more effectively and that production schedules are met.

In the realm of smart home devices, Edge AI has enabled these devices to monitor and manage inventory levels of household essentials such as groceries and cleaning supplies. By using AI algorithms to predict when items need to be replenished and automatically placing orders, these devices can help streamline household inventory management and ensure that supplies are always available when needed.

Overall, Edge AI has transformed inventory management across a wide range of industries, from healthcare monitoring devices to retail analytics. By enabling real-time processing and decision-making at the edge, Edge AI has made inventory management more accurate, efficient, and responsive to changing demands. As the technology continues to advance, we can expect even greater improvements in inventory management practices in the future.

Personalized Marketing Strategies

Personalized marketing strategies are crucial for businesses looking to capitalize on the benefits of Edge AI technology. By leveraging real-time processing capabilities, companies can tailor their marketing efforts to individual customers, delivering personalized content and recommendations at lightning speed. This level of customization not only enhances the customer experience but also increases the likelihood of conversion and customer loyalty.

Edge AI for autonomous drones presents a unique opportunity for personalized marketing strategies. Drones equipped with AI algorithms can gather valuable data about customers' behaviors and preferences, allowing businesses to target specific demographics with personalized advertisements or promotions. This targeted approach can significantly increase the effectiveness of marketing campaigns, leading to higher engagement and conversion rates.

In the realm of industrial robots, Edge AI can revolutionize the way businesses interact with their customers. By analyzing real-time data from production lines and supply chains, companies can optimize their operations to meet the unique needs of individual clients. This level of customization not only improves efficiency but also enhances customer satisfaction, ultimately driving business growth and profitability.

Smart home devices powered by Edge AI offer another avenue for personalized marketing strategies. By collecting and analyzing data on users' daily routines and preferences, these devices can deliver personalized recommendations for products or services that align with their needs. This targeted approach not only increases the relevance of marketing efforts but also fosters stronger connections between businesses and their customers.

In conclusion, personalized marketing strategies are essential for businesses looking to leverage the power of Edge AI technology. By tailoring their marketing efforts to individual customers in real-time, companies can increase engagement, conversion rates, and customer loyalty. Whether it's through autonomous drones, industrial robots, smart home devices, or wearables, businesses can use Edge AI to deliver personalized experiences that set them apart from the competition.

Chapter 9: Edge AI for Predictive Maintenance in Manufacturing

Preventing Downtime with Edge AI

In the fast-paced world of technology, downtime can be a costly and frustrating issue for businesses and individuals alike. This is where Edge AI comes in, offering real-time processing capabilities that can help prevent downtime in a variety of applications. By running AI algorithms locally on devices, Edge AI reduces latency and bandwidth usage, making it ideal for scenarios where immediate decision-making is crucial. From autonomous vehicles to smart cameras and IoT devices, Edge AI is revolutionizing the way we approach real-time processing.

One of the key benefits of Edge AI is its ability to prevent downtime in autonomous drones. By processing data locally on the drone itself, rather than relying on a remote server, Edge AI can help drones make split-second decisions without the need for a constant connection to the cloud. This not only reduces latency but also minimizes the risk of communication errors that could lead to downtime during critical missions.

Industrial robots are another area where Edge AI is making a significant impact in preventing downtime. By leveraging real-time processing capabilities, industrial robots can optimize their operations and make decisions on the fly, without the need for constant communication with a central server. This not only improves efficiency but also reduces the risk of costly downtime in manufacturing processes.

Smart home devices are becoming increasingly popular, but they are also prone to downtime if not properly optimized. Edge AI can help prevent downtime in smart home devices by enabling them to make decisions locally, without the need for constant communication with a cloud server. This not only reduces latency but also improves the overall reliability of smart home devices, ensuring that they are always available when needed.

In conclusion, Edge AI is a powerful tool for preventing downtime in a wide range of applications, from autonomous drones to industrial robots, smart home devices, and beyond. By running AI algorithms locally on devices, Edge AI reduces latency and bandwidth usage, making it ideal for scenarios where immediate decision-making is critical. As technology continues to evolve, Edge AI will play an increasingly important role in preventing downtime and ensuring that our devices are always available when needed.

Predictive Maintenance Algorithms

Predictive maintenance algorithms are a critical component of Edge AI, particularly in the realm of manufacturing. These algorithms utilize machine learning and data analytics to predict when equipment is likely to fail, allowing for proactive maintenance to be performed before any issues occur. By implementing predictive maintenance algorithms, manufacturers can reduce downtime, increase efficiency, and save money on costly repairs.

In the context of autonomous drones, predictive maintenance algorithms play a crucial role in ensuring the safe and reliable operation of these devices. By analyzing data collected from sensors and other sources, these algorithms can predict when components are likely to fail, allowing for preemptive maintenance to be performed. This is essential for ensuring the continued operation of autonomous drones in a variety of applications, from surveillance to delivery.

Industrial robots are another area where predictive maintenance algorithms are particularly valuable. By analyzing data from sensors and other sources, these algorithms can predict when components are likely to fail, allowing for maintenance to be performed before any issues arise.

This is essential for ensuring the continued operation of industrial robots in manufacturing settings, where downtime can be costly and disruptive.

In the realm of smart home devices, predictive maintenance algorithms can help ensure that these devices operate reliably and efficiently. By analyzing data from sensors and other sources, these algorithms can predict when components are likely to fail, allowing for maintenance to be performed proactively. This is essential for ensuring the continued operation of smart home devices, from thermostats to security cameras.

In conclusion, predictive maintenance algorithms are a critical component of Edge AI in a variety of applications, from manufacturing to autonomous drones to smart home devices. By analyzing data and utilizing machine learning, these algorithms can predict when components are likely to fail, allowing for proactive maintenance to be performed. This helps to reduce downtime, increase efficiency, and save money on costly repairs, making predictive maintenance algorithms an essential tool for professionals working in the field of Edge AI.

Cost Savings and Efficiency

Cost savings and efficiency are two key benefits of implementing Edge AI solutions in various industries. By running AI algorithms locally on devices, Edge AI reduces the need for constant data transmission to the cloud, ultimately saving on bandwidth usage and lowering overall costs. This is particularly important for applications requiring real-time processing, such as autonomous vehicles, smart cameras, and IoT devices, where immediate decision-making is critical.

In the realm of autonomous drones, Edge AI plays a crucial role in enabling these devices to make split-second decisions without relying on a constant connection to the cloud. By processing data locally on the drone itself, Edge AI reduces latency and ensures that the drone can navigate and respond to its environment in real-time, ultimately leading to safer and more efficient operations.

Industrial robots also benefit significantly from Edge AI technologies, as they are able to perform complex tasks with minimal latency and without the need for constant cloud connectivity. By running AI algorithms locally on the robot, manufacturers can achieve higher levels of precision and efficiency in their operations, ultimately leading to cost savings and increased productivity.

Smart home devices, wearables, healthcare monitoring devices, agricultural drones, retail analytics systems, and traffic management systems are just a few examples of other applications that can benefit from Edge AI solutions. By processing data locally on these devices, Edge AI reduces the need for constant data transmission to the cloud, ultimately saving on bandwidth usage and ensuring that critical decisions can be made in real-time.

In conclusion, Edge AI offers significant cost savings and efficiency improvements across a wide range of industries and applications. By running AI algorithms locally on devices, Edge AI reduces latency, saves on bandwidth usage, and enables real-time decision-making, ultimately leading to safer, more efficient operations. Whether it's in autonomous vehicles, industrial robots, smart home devices, or healthcare monitoring systems, Edge AI is revolutionizing the way we process data and make decisions in real-time.

Chapter 10: Edge AI for Traffic Management Systems

Smart Cities and Edge AI

Smart cities are rapidly becoming a reality as technology continues to advance and improve. One key aspect of building a smart city is the use of Edge AI, which involves running AI algorithms locally on devices rather than relying on cloud computing. This is particularly important for applications requiring real-time processing, such as autonomous vehicles, smart cameras, and IoT devices. By utilizing Edge AI, cities can reduce latency and bandwidth usage, making it suitable for scenarios where immediate decision-making is critical.

One specific application of Edge AI in smart cities is for autonomous drones. These drones can be used for a variety of tasks, such as monitoring traffic, inspecting infrastructure, or even delivering goods. By processing data locally on the drone itself, rather than sending it back to a central server for analysis, autonomous drones can make decisions quickly and efficiently, enhancing their overall performance and reliability.

Another important use case for Edge AI in smart cities is for industrial robots. These robots are often used in manufacturing facilities to automate tasks and improve efficiency. By running AI algorithms locally on these robots, they can make decisions in real-time, allowing them to adapt to changing conditions and optimize their performance. This not only improves productivity but also reduces the risk of accidents and downtime.

Edge AI also plays a crucial role in smart home devices, wearables, healthcare monitoring devices, agricultural drones, retail analytics, predictive maintenance in manufacturing, traffic management systems, and cybersecurity on IoT devices. By processing data locally on these devices, rather than relying on cloud computing, these applications can operate more efficiently and securely. This is particularly important for scenarios where data privacy and security are paramount, such as healthcare and cybersecurity.

In conclusion, Edge AI is a critical component of building smart cities that are efficient, secure, and responsive. By running AI algorithms locally on devices, rather than relying on cloud computing, cities can reduce latency, bandwidth usage, and improve decision-making in real-time. From autonomous drones to industrial robots to smart home devices, Edge AI has the potential to transform how cities operate and improve the quality of life for their residents. For professionals working in the field of Edge AI, understanding its applications in smart cities is essential for developing innovative solutions that will shape the future of urban living.

Traffic Flow Optimization

Traffic Flow Optimization is a critical aspect of modern transportation systems, especially in urban areas where congestion is a common issue. By leveraging Edge AI technology, traffic flow can be optimized in real-time, leading to smoother and more efficient traffic patterns. This is particularly important for applications requiring immediate decision-making, such as autonomous vehicles and smart cameras, where delays can have serious consequences.

Edge AI plays a crucial role in optimizing traffic flow by enabling devices to process data locally, rather than relying on cloud computing. This reduces latency and bandwidth usage, making it ideal for scenarios where quick decision-making is essential. For autonomous vehicles, Edge AI can analyze traffic conditions in real-time and adjust routes accordingly, ensuring safe and efficient navigation. Similarly, smart cameras equipped with Edge AI can monitor traffic patterns and detect anomalies, allowing for proactive interventions to prevent congestion.

In the realm of traffic management systems, Edge AI offers a range of benefits, from reducing response times to improving overall system efficiency. By processing data at the edge, traffic management devices can quickly analyze traffic flow, identify bottlenecks, and implement dynamic traffic control measures to alleviate congestion. This real-time processing capability is essential for ensuring smooth traffic flow and enhancing the overall effectiveness of traffic management systems.

Edge AI is also being utilized in predictive maintenance for manufacturing, retail analytics, cybersecurity on IoT devices, and healthcare monitoring devices. These applications all require real-time processing capabilities to make timely decisions and optimize system performance. By harnessing the power of Edge AI, professionals can ensure that their systems operate efficiently, securely, and effectively, even in high-pressure environments.

In conclusion, Edge AI is revolutionizing traffic flow optimization and other critical applications by enabling real-time processing on devices. By leveraging Edge AI technology, professionals can improve traffic management systems, enhance autonomous vehicle navigation, and optimize various other systems requiring immediate decision-making. With its ability to reduce latency and bandwidth usage, Edge AI is a game-changer for industries where quick data analysis is paramount.

Real-Time Decision Making

Real-time decision making is a critical aspect of Edge AI, particularly in applications such as autonomous vehicles, smart cameras, and IoT devices. The ability to run AI algorithms locally on devices reduces latency and bandwidth usage, making it ideal for scenarios where immediate decision-making is essential. This is in contrast to traditional cloud computing, which may introduce delays that are unacceptable in time-sensitive situations.

One area where real-time decision making is crucial is in autonomous drones. These drones rely on Edge AI to quickly process data from their surroundings and make split-second decisions to navigate safely and efficiently. Without real-time processing capabilities, autonomous drones would not be able to react quickly enough to obstacles or changing conditions, putting both the drone and any people or property in the vicinity at risk.

In the realm of industrial robots, real-time decision making is essential for ensuring safety and efficiency in manufacturing processes. Edge AI enables robots to quickly analyze data from their sensors and make adjustments to their movements in real-time. This not only improves the speed and accuracy of manufacturing processes but also reduces the risk of accidents or errors that could result from delayed decision-making.

Smart home devices, such as security cameras and thermostats, also benefit from Edge AI's real-time processing capabilities. By running AI algorithms locally on these devices, they can quickly respond to events such as motion detection or changes in temperature without needing to send data to the cloud and wait for a response. This not only reduces latency but also enhances privacy and security by keeping sensitive data within the user's home network.

In conclusion, real-time decision making is a fundamental aspect of Edge AI that is crucial for a wide range of applications, from autonomous vehicles to healthcare monitoring devices. By processing data locally on devices, Edge AI enables immediate decision-making that is essential for scenarios where delays are unacceptable. As Edge AI continues to evolve and expand into new industries, the importance of real-time processing capabilities will only grow, driving innovation and advancements in a wide range of fields.

Chapter 11: Edge AI for Cybersecurity on IoT Devices

Securing IoT Networks with Edge AI

As the Internet of Things (IoT) continues to grow and expand, the need for secure networks becomes increasingly important. With the rise of Edge AI, which involves running AI algorithms locally on devices rather than relying on cloud computing, securing IoT networks has become more efficient and effective. Edge AI is particularly crucial for applications requiring real-time processing, such as autonomous vehicles, smart cameras, and IoT devices. By reducing latency and bandwidth usage, Edge AI ensures immediate decision-making, making it suitable for scenarios where real-time data processing is critical.

One of the key areas where Edge AI plays a significant role in securing IoT networks is in autonomous drones. These drones require real-time processing capabilities to navigate and make decisions on the fly. With Edge AI, drones can analyze data locally, reducing the risk of data breaches or delays in decision-making due to connectivity issues. This ensures that autonomous drones can operate safely and securely in various environments.

Industrial robots are another area where Edge AI is essential for securing IoT networks. These robots rely on real-time data processing to perform complex tasks in manufacturing and other industries. By using Edge AI, industrial robots can analyze data locally and make decisions quickly, reducing the risk of cyberattacks or data breaches. This ensures that industrial robots can operate efficiently and securely without compromising on performance.

Smart home devices are becoming increasingly popular, but they also pose security risks if not properly protected. Edge AI plays a crucial role in securing IoT networks for smart home devices by enabling local data processing and decision-making. This reduces the risk of data breaches or cyberattacks, ensuring that smart home devices can operate securely and protect the privacy of users.

In conclusion, Edge AI is a powerful tool for securing IoT networks in various industries and applications. From autonomous drones to industrial robots, smart home devices, wearables, and more, Edge AI enables real-time processing and decision-making locally, reducing latency and bandwidth usage. This ensures that IoT devices can operate securely and efficiently, even in scenarios where immediate decision-making is critical. By implementing Edge AI in IoT networks, professionals can enhance security, protect data privacy, and improve overall performance in various industries and applications.

Threat Detection and Prevention

Threat detection and prevention are critical components of Edge AI systems, especially in scenarios where immediate decision-making is crucial. With the rise of autonomous vehicles, smart cameras, and IoT devices, the need for real-time processing has never been more pressing. Edge AI offers a solution by running AI algorithms locally on devices, reducing latency and bandwidth usage. This allows for quicker responses to potential threats, ensuring the safety and security of users and their surroundings.

One key application of Edge AI in threat detection is in the realm of autonomous drones. These drones rely on real-time processing to navigate their surroundings and make split-second decisions to avoid obstacles or potential dangers. By incorporating threat detection and prevention algorithms into their systems, autonomous drones can operate more safely and efficiently, minimizing the risk of accidents or collisions.

In the realm of industrial robots, Edge AI plays a crucial role in ensuring the safety of workers and equipment. By detecting potential threats in real-time, such as malfunctioning machinery or hazardous conditions, industrial robots can take immediate action to prevent accidents and mitigate risks. This not only protects the well-being of workers but also improves the overall efficiency and productivity of the manufacturing process.

Smart home devices also benefit from Edge AI in threat detection and prevention. By running AI algorithms locally on devices such as security cameras or smart locks, threats such as break-ins or unauthorized access can be detected and addressed immediately. This provides homeowners with peace of mind knowing that their homes are protected and secure, even when they are away.

In conclusion, Edge AI is a powerful tool for threat detection and prevention in a wide range of applications, from autonomous drones to smart home devices. By enabling real-time processing and decision-making locally on devices, Edge AI reduces latency and improves response times to potential threats. This not only enhances the safety and security of users but also improves the efficiency and effectiveness of various systems and processes. As the demand for real-time processing continues to grow, Edge AI will play an increasingly important role in ensuring the safety and security of our interconnected world.

Compliance and Best Practices

Compliance and best practices are crucial aspects of implementing Edge AI solutions in various industries. With the increasing use of AI algorithms on devices at the edge, it is important to ensure that these solutions adhere to regulatory requirements and industry standards. This is particularly important for applications requiring real-time processing, such as autonomous vehicles, smart cameras, and IoT devices, where immediate decision-making is critical.

When it comes to compliance, organizations must consider data privacy and security regulations, as well as ethical considerations related to the use of AI algorithms. It is important to implement data protection measures, such as encryption and access controls, to safeguard sensitive information processed by Edge AI solutions. Additionally, organizations should adhere to industry standards and best practices to ensure the reliability and performance of their Edge AI systems.

In the context of Edge AI for autonomous drones, compliance with aviation regulations is essential to ensure safe and efficient operations. Organizations must adhere to guidelines set forth by regulatory bodies, such as the Federal Aviation Administration (FAA), to mitigate risks associated with drone operations. Best practices for autonomous drones include real-time processing of sensor data to enable obstacle detection and collision avoidance, as well as the ability to make split-second decisions to navigate complex environments.

In the realm of Edge AI for industrial robots, compliance with safety regulations is paramount to protect workers and prevent accidents in manufacturing facilities. Organizations must follow guidelines established by occupational safety authorities to ensure the safe operation of AI-powered robots on the factory floor. Best practices for industrial robots include real-time monitoring of equipment performance and predictive maintenance to prevent costly downtime and optimize production efficiency.

In conclusion, compliance and best practices play a crucial role in the successful implementation of Edge AI solutions across various industries. By following regulatory requirements and industry standards, organizations can ensure the security, reliability, and performance of their AI algorithms running at the edge. Whether it is for autonomous vehicles, industrial robots, smart home devices, wearables, healthcare monitoring devices, agricultural drones, retail analytics, predictive maintenance in manufacturing, traffic management systems, or cybersecurity on IoT devices, compliance and best practices are essential for leveraging the full potential of Edge AI technologies.

Chapter 12: Conclusion and Future Outlook

Key Takeaways

1. Edge AI is a revolutionary technology that involves running AI algorithms locally on devices rather than relying on cloud computing. This is particularly important for applications requiring real-time processing, such as autonomous vehicles, smart cameras, and IoT devices. By processing data at the edge, latency is reduced and bandwidth usage is minimized, making it suitable for scenarios where immediate decision-making is critical.

2. Edge AI is transforming industries such as autonomous drones, industrial robots, smart home devices, wearables, healthcare monitoring devices, agricultural drones, retail analytics, predictive maintenance in manufacturing, traffic management systems, and cybersecurity on IoT devices. These applications benefit from the speed and efficiency of edge AI, enabling them to make real-time decisions and responses without relying on a cloud connection.

3. Edge AI for autonomous drones allows them to navigate complex environments and make split-second decisions without relying on a constant internet connection. This is essential for applications such as search and rescue missions, surveillance, and delivery services where immediate responses are crucial.

4. Edge AI for industrial robots enables them to perform tasks with precision and efficiency, reducing the need for human intervention and increasing productivity. By processing data locally, these robots can adapt to changing conditions in real-time, improving overall performance and safety in manufacturing environments.

5. In conclusion, edge AI is a game-changer for professionals across various industries, offering real-time processing capabilities that enhance efficiency, speed, and accuracy. By leveraging edge AI technology, businesses can unlock new opportunities for innovation and growth in autonomous systems, IoT devices, smart home applications, healthcare monitoring, agriculture, retail, manufacturing, traffic management, and cybersecurity. Stay ahead of the curve by incorporating edge AI solutions into your professional toolkit and experience the transformative power of real-time processing at the edge.

Emerging Trends in Edge AI

As technology continues to advance, emerging trends in Edge AI are becoming increasingly prevalent in various industries. Edge AI, which involves running AI algorithms locally on devices rather than relying on cloud computing, is particularly important for applications requiring real-time processing. This includes autonomous vehicles, smart cameras, and IoT devices, where immediate decision-making is critical. By reducing latency and bandwidth usage, Edge AI is revolutionizing the way these technologies operate, making them more efficient and responsive than ever before.

One niche that is seeing significant growth in the utilization of Edge AI is autonomous drones. These drones require real-time processing capabilities to navigate obstacles, avoid collisions, and make split-second decisions. Edge AI enables these drones to operate autonomously and safely, without the need for constant communication with a centralized server. This trend is expected to continue as the demand for autonomous drones grows in industries such as agriculture, surveillance, and delivery services.

Industrial robots are another niche where Edge AI is making a big impact. By running AI algorithms locally on the robots themselves, manufacturers can increase efficiency, improve precision, and reduce the risk of downtime. Edge AI allows these robots to adapt to changing conditions in real-time, making them more flexible and versatile in a fast-paced production environment. This trend is reshaping the manufacturing industry, paving the way for a new era of smart factories powered by Edge AI technology.

Smart home devices are also benefiting from the advancements in Edge AI. From smart thermostats to security cameras, these devices can now process data locally to make intelligent decisions without relying on cloud servers. This not only improves response times but also enhances privacy and security for homeowners. With the rise of the Internet of Things (IoT), Edge AI is becoming increasingly important in creating a seamless and interconnected smart home ecosystem that is efficient, secure, and user-friendly.

In conclusion, Edge AI is revolutionizing the way we interact with technology in various industries. From healthcare monitoring devices to agricultural drones, retail analytics to traffic management systems, Edge AI is enabling real-time processing and decision-making at the edge of the network. As these trends continue to evolve, professionals in these niches must stay informed and adapt to the changing landscape of Edge AI to stay competitive and innovative in their respective fields.

Recommendations for Professionals in the Field

When working in the field of Edge AI, there are several key recommendations that professionals should keep in mind to ensure success in their projects. First and foremost, it is crucial to stay updated on the latest advancements and trends in Edge AI technology. This fast-paced industry is constantly evolving, so professionals must continuously educate themselves on new tools, techniques, and best practices to stay ahead of the curve.

Secondly, professionals should prioritize security when implementing Edge AI solutions. With the rise of IoT devices and interconnected systems, the risk of cyber attacks and data breaches is higher than ever. It is essential to implement robust security measures to protect sensitive data and ensure the integrity of AI algorithms running on edge devices.

Moreover, professionals should focus on optimizing the performance of Edge AI algorithms to achieve real-time processing capabilities. This involves fine-tuning algorithms, minimizing latency, and maximizing efficiency to deliver fast and accurate results. By optimizing performance, professionals can enhance the overall user experience and improve the effectiveness of Edge AI applications.

In addition, collaboration and communication are key components of success in the field of Edge AI. Professionals should work closely with cross-functional teams, including data scientists, engineers, and domain experts, to leverage their diverse expertise and perspectives. By fostering collaboration, professionals can drive innovation, solve complex problems, and deliver impactful solutions in Edge AI applications.

Lastly, professionals should always prioritize ethical considerations when developing and deploying Edge AI solutions. It is important to ensure transparency, fairness, and accountability in AI algorithms to mitigate bias, discrimination, and unintended consequences. By upholding ethical standards, professionals can build trust with users, regulators, and stakeholders, and pave the way for responsible and sustainable adoption of Edge AI technology.

www.ingramcontent.com/pod-product-compliance
Lightning Source LLC
Chambersburg PA
CBHW082241220526
45479CB00005B/1301